HOW THE ANIMALS CAME TO NORTH AMERICA

"May describes how some animals evolved in North America
and how others traveled there by way of land bridges that
formed after the single prehistoric continent of Pangaea
broke apart...a simple, clear explanation of the subject."

<u>The Booklist</u>

"A seasoned author of science and nature books, Ms. M
offers this intelligent and comprehensive account of
wild creatures to be found in the United States and
Canada."

<u>Publishers Weekly</u>

HOLIDAY HOUSE INC., 18 EAST 56th STREET N.Y., N.Y.

How the Animals
Came to North America

How the Animals
Came to North America

By Julian May

Illustrated by Lorence F. Bjorklund

HOLIDAY HOUSE · NEW YORK

LIBRARY OF CONGRESS CATALOGING IN PUBLICATION DATA

May, Julian.
    How the animals came to North America.

    SUMMARY: Describes the migration of animal life
to the North American continent and its subsequent
evolution.
    1. Animal migration—Juvenile literature.
2. Evolution—Juvenile literature. 3. Zoogeography
—North America—Juvenile literature. [1. Animal
migration. 2. Evolution] I. Bjorklund,
Lorence F., illus. II. Title.
QL754.M33   569'.097   73–17145
ISBN O–8234–0234–7

AUTHOR'S NOTE

The study of animal distribution and spread over the world is called zoogeography. The slow spread of a species into a new range is quite different from annual migration—the yearly round trips taken by some animals. The migrating animal takes a trip and returns to its place of origin.

North America has all kinds of animals.
There are tame ones and wild ones,
large ones and small ones,
animals of the land, the water, and the air.
Where did they all come from?

The tame animals came to America with man.
The first settlers from Europe brought
cats and dogs, horses and cattle,
sheep, pigs, goats, and chickens.
Most of these animals got here about 450 years ago.

8

Long before the European settlers came,
ancestors of the Indians came
to the New World from eastern Asia.
They probably brought tame dogs with them.
This happened at least 40,000 years ago.

It isn't hard to find out where tame animals
came from. But what about wild animals?
Have they been here always?
Some have.
Scientists say some animals evolved here.

PREHISTORIC
PRONGHORN

Evolution of the pronghorn antelope

Millions of years ago,
early forms of the pronghorn antelope
lived in North America.
As time passed, these animals evolved,
or changed very slowly,
into the pronghorns of today.
The pronghorns are real "native Americans."
They never lived anywhere else.

THE PRONGHORN
OF TODAY

Evolution is the slow changing of
one animal form into others.

TURKEY

There are a few other kinds of animals
that are found only in North America.
Scientists can tell which
animals evolved here
by studying their fossils—
traces of animal bodies
left in ancient rocks.

CHIPMUNK

These animal families evolved in
North America.
Fossils can tell us what ancient animals
looked like. Sometimes fossils show how one
animal evolved into another one.

RATTLESNAKE

All through earth's history,
animals have evolved.
Some ancient kinds of animals died out.
Others kept on living beside the newer kinds.
Today, North America has both ancient
and newer kinds of animals living together.

The cockroach is a very ancient insect. It has
lived in North America (and other parts of the
world) for 300 million years. The monarch butterfly
is probably less than one million years old.

13

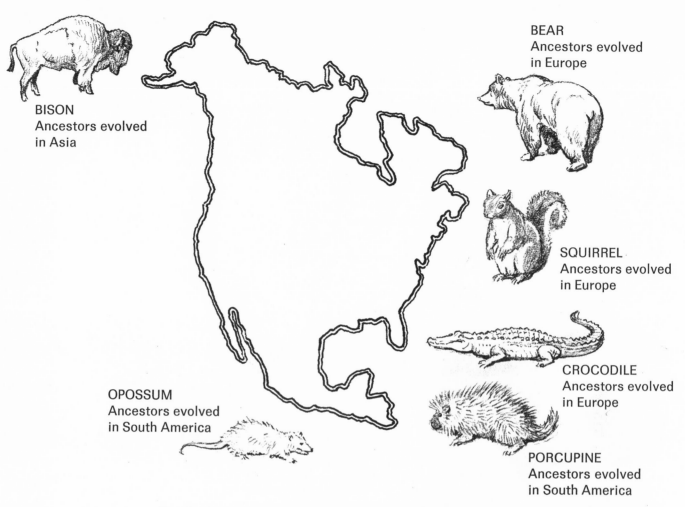

BISON
Ancestors evolved
in Asia

BEAR
Ancestors evolved
in Europe

SQUIRREL
Ancestors evolved
in Europe

CROCODILE
Ancestors evolved
in Europe

OPOSSUM
Ancestors evolved
in South America

PORCUPINE
Ancestors evolved
in South America

Evolution can explain how some kinds
of animals came to live in North America.
But it cannot explain all of them.
Fossils show that some animal families evolved
on other continents. Then they spread here.
This has been going on for a long time.
How did the animals get here?

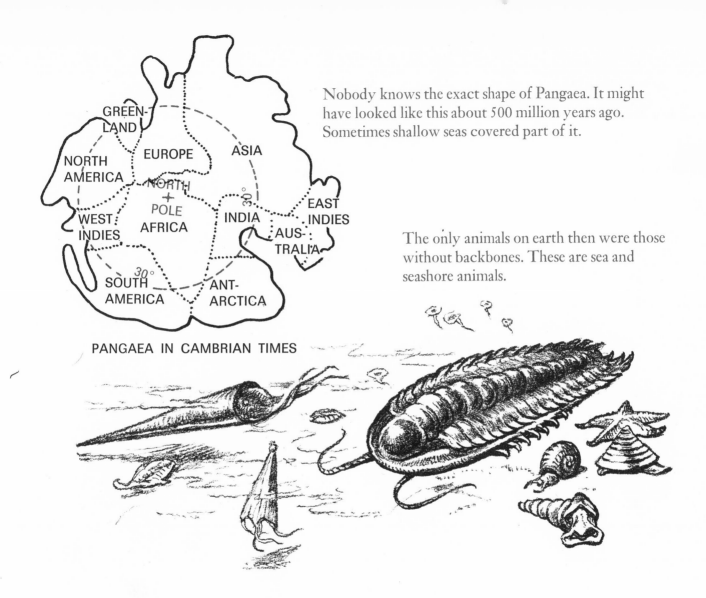

Nobody knows the exact shape of Pangaea. It might have looked like this about 500 million years ago. Sometimes shallow seas covered part of it.

PANGAEA IN CAMBRIAN TIMES

The only animals on earth then were those without backbones. These are sea and seashore animals.

In the very earliest days of the earth,
animal travel overland was easy.
All of the continents were joined together.
Earth had a single huge continent, Pangaea.

Animal life in Laurasia about 135 million years ago. Fossils of these animals occur in both North America and Eurasia.

DINOSAUR

TRICERATOPS

Then Pangaea started breaking apart. The southern part broke off from the northern part. This took a very long time. All that time, animals were evolving. Many of them spread from place to place.

NORTH POLE

ASIA

NORTH AMERICA

EUROPE

SOUTH AMERICA

AFRICA

INDIA

AUS-TRALIA

ANTARCTICA

SOUTH POLE

EQUATOR

NORTH POLE

N.A.

EUROPE

LAURASIA

AFRICA

SOUTH AMERICA

GONDWANALAND

INDIA

ANT-ARCTICA

AUSTRALIA

SOUTH POLE

About 300 million years ago, Pangaea looked like this.

About 135 million years ago, Pangaea split into Laurasia and Gondwanaland.

AMPHICYON

EOHIPPUS

BOTHRIODON

EUSMILUS

Animal life in Laurasia about 35 million years ago, when Europe and North America were still joined.

Much later, both land masses broke up again. The northern mass became Eurasia and North America. The southern mass became Africa, Australia, Antarctica, and South America.

About 35 million years ago, the continents moved to about the positions they have now. But the land bridges between continents were different from those of today.

NORTH AMERICA

EUROPE

ASIA

AFRICA

SOUTH AMERICA

AUSTRALIA

ANTARCTICA

17

ANAS DUCKS

Animal travel became much harder as the
continents moved apart. Flying animals
and swimmers could go from continent to
continent—if they were strong.
Land animals were stopped by the sea.

PALEOMASTODON

While the continents drifted apart
30 million years ago, ducks much like
today's mallards evolved in Asia and spread
around the world. The otter-like potamotherium
spread from Europe to North America by
swimming. Its descendants became the fur seals.

POTAMOTHERIUM

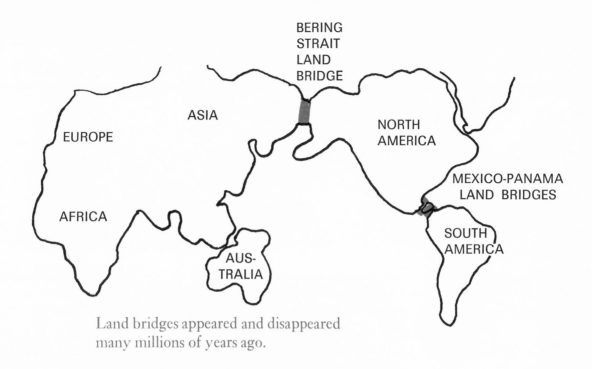

BERING
STRAIT
LAND
BRIDGE

ASIA

EUROPE

NORTH
AMERICA

AFRICA

MEXICO-PANAMA
LAND BRIDGES

AUS-
TRALIA

SOUTH
AMERICA

Land bridges appeared and disappeared
many millions of years ago.

The continents did not all move far apart.
North America and Asia were very close.
And South America was not very far
from North America. As years went by,
land bridges began to form.
Some were made of soil washed from the land by rain.
Some were made when mountains thrust up
from the sea bottom.

The land bridges did not always last
a long time. But as long as they existed, some
animals were able to cross them in both directions.

South America to North America

OPOSSUM

ARMADILLO

PORCUPINE

These animals crossed the
land bridges at various times
between five million and
25 million years ago.

Asia to North America

SCIURUS
SQUIRREL

LEPUS HARE

MARTEN

MASTODON

North America to Asia

ANCHITHERIUM HORSE

CAMEL

LYNX

20

OLD-WORLD
WILD PIG

These members of the pig family
evolved separately after Laurasia
split apart. They probably never
traveled because they could not
stand very cold weather along
the northern land bridge.

Some kinds of animals are not travelers.
Stay-at-home animals are usually those
that cannot survive a change in climate
or a new kind of food. There are many
animals like this living today.

NEW-WORLD
PECCARY

OPOSSUM, A "LIVING FOSSIL"—
ABOUT 100 MILLION YEARS OLD

Not all of the animal travelers of the past
still live in North America.
Many of them evolved, or changed, into new forms.
Others died out. They became extinct.
A few animals have changed their form very little
over the ages. They are "living fossils," so to speak.

PIKA, AN ANIMAL SOMEWHAT LIKE
A RABBIT—ABOUT 30 MILLION YEARS OLD

FOX SQUIRREL, THE BIGGEST
TREE SQUIRREL—ABOUT 20 MILLION
YEARS OLD

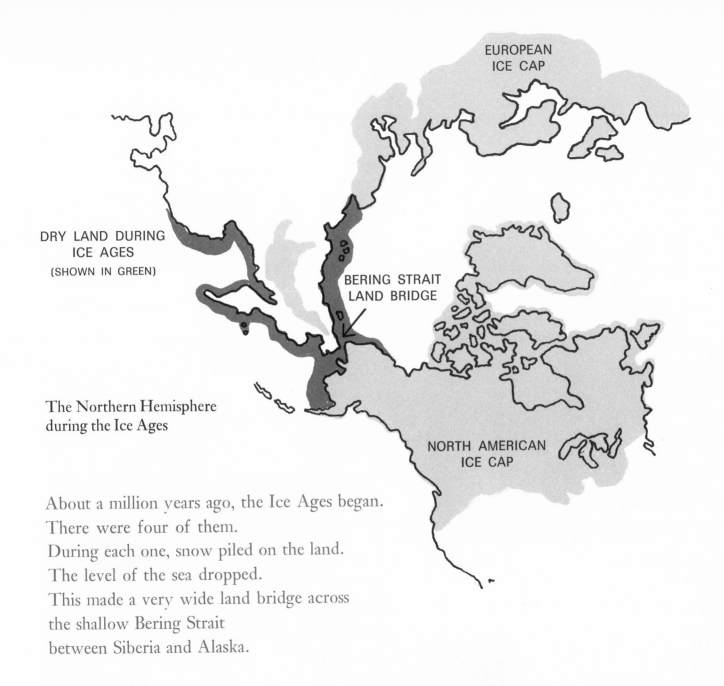

EUROPEAN
ICE CAP

DRY LAND DURING
ICE AGES
(SHOWN IN GREEN)

BERING STRAIT
LAND BRIDGE

The Northern Hemisphere
during the Ice Ages

NORTH AMERICAN
ICE CAP

About a million years ago, the Ice Ages began.
There were four of them.
During each one, snow piled on the land.
The level of the sea dropped.
This made a very wide land bridge across
the shallow Bering Strait
between Siberia and Alaska.

During the First Ice Age, bears, deer, beavers, and many other animals crossed from Asia to North America. The climate was cold along the land bridge, but it was not much worse than the climate in middle Canada today.

The animals that came over had to wait for the ice to melt before they could go southward from Alaska.

MULE
DEER

BEAR

STEPPE MAMMOTH

BEAVER

LEMMING

24

IMPERIAL MAMMOTH

BISON

REINDEER

The North American ice cap was huge.
When it melted, it left empty land.
The invading animals multiplied
and swarmed southward.
There they continued to evolve.

When the ice cap melted,
the northern land bridge was covered by water.
Then a Second Ice Age began about 500,000 years ago.
The sea fell again. Once more animals could
cross on dry land between Asia and North America.

The black bear entered North America
during the Second Ice Age. It probably
came from China.

26

There is a lot still to be learned
about animal travels during the Ice Ages.
Scientists are discovering new fossils
that fill in blank places in the fossil record.
Meanwhile, we know a lot about the travels of
some large animals—and not as much about the
travels of smaller animals and birds.

The bones of small animals are easily
destroyed by scavengers—animals that
find and eat dead creatures. Large bones
survive more easily and become fossils.

The Third Ice Age started about 250,000
years ago. The sea sank to its lowest point.
It was very cold.
The first Old World animals to cross the
Bering land bridge were arctic kinds
that did not mind the climate.

MUSK OXEN

WOOLLY MAMMOTH

REINDEER

TIMBER WOLVES

ERMINE

MOOSE

ELK

GRAY FOX

OTTER

WOLVERINE

RED FOX

Later, as the ice cap shrank
and it became warmer, forest animals crossed.
There were moose, elk, wolverines, and otters.
The red fox of the Old World joined its cousin,
the gray fox of the New World.

The warm times ended once again.
The Fourth Ice Age started about
80,000 years ago. More animals came from
Asia to North America: the arctic fox,
the grizzly bear and polar bear,
snowshoe hares, mountain goats and sheep.
The yak and saiga antelope came, too.
But they later became extinct.

POLAR BEAR

GRIZZLY BEAR

MOUNTAIN GOAT

BIGHORN SHEEP

SNOWSHOE
HARE

ARCTIC FOX

31

The most important animal traveler of all
came from Asia during the Fourth Ice Age.
Man.
He followed his food animals over the land bridge
without even knowing he came to a new world.

It was probably man the hunter
that killed off American elephants,
camels, and horses—as well as the
yaks and saiga antelopes.

The last Ice Age ended
about 8,000 years ago.
This put an end to the last great
arrival of animals.

Walruses and polar bears still travel
from Siberia to North America,
drifting on the arctic ice.

Why did the animals travel at all?
Plant-eaters usually travel
because there are too many of them.
When more young animals grow up in one area,
they must travel in order to find enough to eat.
They move into any place where there is food and room.

BISON

Plant-eaters must stop traveling when they reach a place
where their plant food does not grow.

Meat-eaters—such as cats and dogs—
must follow the animals they hunt.
When plant-eaters travel, meat-eaters follow.

The arctic fox follows
traveling hares and lemmings.

And then there are the natural wanderers, the animals that seem to travel because they like to. Many of these eat both plants and animals. They include opossums, raccoons, bears . . . and man.

Bears are great wanderers. Even today they travel long distances and sometimes come into towns.

Some animals that came to North America
long ago still live here today.
Others have vanished forever.
The fate of those that are left
depends upon mankind.
For now it is man—not nature—who decides
what animals travel from continent to continent.

INDEX

animals, Arctic, 28, 30-31
    evolving, 10, 11, 12, 13, 14, 22, 25
    extinct, 13, 22, 30-31
    flying, 18, 27
    native American, 11, 12, 29
    on other continents, 14, 16, 18, 20, 21, 24, 26
    swimming, 18
    tame, 7, 8, 9, 10
Arctic fox, 30-31

bears, 24, 30-31, 36
beavers, 24
birds, 27

camels, 32
cats, 8, 35
cattle, 8

change of climate, 21
change of food, 21, 32, 34, 35, 36
chickens, 8
climate, 21; *see also* Ice Ages
continents (general), 14, 15, 16, 17, 18, 19, 20, 23, 24, 26, 30-31, 37
    Africa, 17
    Antarctica, 17
    Asia, 9, 19, 20
    Australia, 17
    Eurasia, 17, 19, 23, 26, 28, 29, 30-31
    North America, 7, 13, 14, 19, 23, 24, 25, 26, 27, 28, 29, 30-31, 32, 37
    South America, 17, 19

deer, 24
dogs, 8, 9, 35

elephants, 32
elk, 29
European settlers, 8, 9

First Ice Age, 24
fossils, 12, 14, 27
Fourth Ice Age, 30-31

gray fox, 29

horses, 8, 32

Ice Ages, 23, 24, 26, 28, 29, 30-31
ice cap, 25, 26
Indians, ancestors of, 9

land bridges, 19, 20, 23, 24, 26, 28,
        29, 30-31, 32
"living" fossils, 22

man, 32, 36, 37
moose, 29
mountains, 19

opossums, 36
otters, 29

Pangaea, 15, 16, 17, 18, 19
pigs, 8
pronghorn antelope, 11

raccoons, 36
rain, 19
red fox, 29

saiga antelope, 30-31
sea, 18, 19, 23, 26, 28
Second Ice Age, 26
sheep, 8
snow, 23
soil, 19

Third Ice Age, 28, 29

wolverines, 29

yaks, 30-31